Overcoming Imposter Syndrome

Six Steps to Reclaiming Your Confidence
and Empowering Other Women to Do the Same

Beth Caldwell

Pennsylvania Family Publishing

Overcoming Imposter Syndrome:
Six Steps to Reclaiming Your Confidence and
Empowering Other Women to Do the Same
Copyright ©2024
By Beth Caldwell

Pennsylvania Family Publishing
CoachBethCaldwell.com

The intent of the author is to offer advice and information of a general nature to women who want to be influential leaders at work, at home, and in the community. Advice given is offered solely from the personal experiences of the author and is provided without specific knowledge or training in mental health or medical treatments. The information contained in this book is not intended as a substitute for the knowledge, skill, and judgment of qualified psychiatrists, psychologists, physicians, health care, holistic, wellness, or other practitioners or professionals. Always seek the advice of a qualified health or mental health professional before making important changes or decisions.

Note from the author: Within this book, there are examples and stories from various client interactions taken from my experience as a corporate trainer and business consultant. To ensure their privacy and confidentiality, their names and details have been changed.

ISBN: 978-1-956989-27-4
Interior and Cover Design by Fariha Akter Mim

Dedication

To the little girl in each one of us.
May she be strong, happy, bold, and free
from the imposter

Contents

ALERT:

When self-confidence grows, incredible possibilities emerge. You'll embrace new challenges, conquer old fears, and inspire others to step beyond comfort zones with a positive mindset, fostering a ripple effect of personal growth and achievement.

Beth Caldwell

1
What is Imposter Syndrome?

"I cannot believe they chose ME for this job."
"Even though I prepare well for exams, I am certain I have failed each one."
"I don't speak up in meetings because I don't want to be embarrassed."
"I don't apply for jobs unless I'm over-qualified."
"I know my idea is better than others, but it's not perfect...yet."
"I'll get more qualifications, then apply for a promotion."

Have you ever gotten a job or promotion and felt it must be a mistake?
Have you ever said to yourself, "Surely they know there is someone more qualified?
Do you do this even though you are very competent and qualified?

This is Imposter Syndrome. If you're unfamiliar with it, Imposter Syndrome is a heavily researched scientific and social topic frequently discussed in leadership forums. Its classic definition is the persistent inability to believe that one's success is deserved or has been achieved as the result of one's efforts. Women, in particular, struggle with this.

Approximately 25-30% of high achievers suffer from Imposter Syndrome and a staggering 70% state that they have experienced it at some point in their lifetimes. According to Psychology Today, people with imposter syndrome feel like frauds despite abundant evidence of their success. Instead of acknowledging their capabilities and efforts, they often attribute their accomplishments to external or transient causes, such as luck, good timing, karma, or fate.

Given that imposter syndrome is an emotion-based phenomenon, it's not readily apparent when we are struggling with it, why we do it, and what to do about it.

I've been training women to overcome imposter syndrome for nearly ten years, but it wasn't until recently that I realized the need for more women to get this message. Last summer, my family and I were attending a high school graduation at the home of a colleague. The house was grand and modern, filled with the best furniture and decor. Every piece of furniture and accessory appeared to be brand new. It was so perfect that it seemed unwise to sit or disturb anything, so I found myself standing in the family room admiring the dozens of beautifully framed photos strategically placed around it.

A young family arrived: Mom, Dad, and three daughters under the age of ten, all impeccably dressed. Mom seemed tense. The girls looked uncomfortable and afraid to move or muss their matching outfits. Dad dashed outside to join the men gathering around the volleyball nets. As she entered the room, the mom took in my appearance from head to toe (she easily out-styled me) and then turned to the mantle to look at the photos on display.

"Mariah, Michaela, Mackenzie, come and look!" she

gasped aloud. The girls obediently went to their mother.

"Now THIS!" she exclaimed, pointing at one of the elegantly framed photos, "This is the type of wedding I want for you three. Imagine getting married in an actual CASTLE. Wouldn't that be wonderful?"

The young girls immediately began to chatter about their wedding fantasies, comparing thoughts of beach weddings versus castle weddings.

This encounter prompted me to be in observation mode over the next few months, noticing how often women set out to outshine one another, going over the imaginary checklists in their heads, and feeling the need to constantly compare, keep up, and have children that outperform. I noticed women doing this to each other and themselves. These habits are where the feeling of being an imposter begins: not being good enough, pretty enough, thin enough, or not having enough.

The women I work with today deal with imposter syndrome at work, home, and even at volunteer positions in the community. Many of them grew up with messages like this:

- Boys are good at math, girls are better at reading and crafts
- Being pretty is more important than being smart
- Being different is dangerous
- People prefer girls who are quiet, helpful, thin, etc.
- Women make excellent caregivers
- Girls are too emotional to be leaders

3

- Let someone smarter/stronger do that for you

Even if we KNOW intellectually that these messages
are not valid, they have become internalized and
often
resurface later in life.

Here's what happens: Women tend to:

- Stay quiet
- Settle for less
- Avoid conflict
- Avoid attention
- Wait to be asked
- Not expect a raise
- Not ask for promotions
- Keep their dreams hidden
- Feel silly about wanting more
- Avoid being different
- Stay in unhappy jobs and relationships
- Prioritize other's needs over their own

Numerous research studies explain why we do this. This
book does not include science, statistics, or studies.
(To understand how Imposter Syndrome happens,
research evolutionary psychology, primal fears,
caveman brain, and brain functions of the amygdala
and limbic system.) Instead, I have outlined six simple
steps for overcoming Imposter Syndrome forever.

HOW TO STOP THE PROGRAMMING

To begin, consider how often you hear (or ask, or are asked) questions like this about the relationships in your life:

1. Do you have a boyfriend?
2. Do you have a date for the prom?
3. Are you planning to get married?
4. What kind of wedding do you think you'll have?
5. Why aren't you married yet?
6. Where is your husband?
7. When are you going to have children?
8. When are you going to have another child?
9. When is that child of yours going to get married?
10. When are you going to have grandchildren?

What is your initial response or internalized feeling when asked these questions? For many, the realization that young girls, even today, are being unintentionally programmed to please others by catching a husband instead of creating a fulfilling life feels a bit frustrating and embarrassing.

You'll come to know me as a truth-teller. The truth is that weddings and babies were celebrated accomplishments for centuries, and they still are! Women today (in most countries) can also enjoy education, careers, military service, travel, independence, and more. You may feel judgmental or defensive when you notice yourself or others making inquiries like the ones above. Please resist the urge to judge yourself or others.Instead, when you hear young girls or grown women being asked these types of personal questions, become a role model for others by asking better ones.

Here are some examples:

1. Do you like to read?
2. Do you like sports?
3. What is the best thing about graduation parties?
4. Which do you like better, beaches or mountains?
5. If you could have lunch with anyone, who would it be?
6. Do you think animals can communicate?
7. Are you thinking about college?
8. I'm impressed with your career so far. What's next for you?
9. What's happened since we last met?
10. Where would you go if you could visit any country in the world tomorrow?

The first set of questions are the ones we've been conditioned to ask and can result in shame, awkwardness, and discomfort. The second set conditions others to think, respond, and engage. When asked, they are likely to result in sparkling eyes, smiling, and connection.

HELP THOSE WHO ARE PRE-PROGRAMMED

The workforce is filled with women who have been programmed to stay small and quiet. By providing a work environment that is safe and supportive, we can show all employees that it's acceptable to share their thoughts and ideas. In many forward-thinking companies, this trend is not only accepted, it's expected.

If you or someone you work with someone is struggling with the imposter, I recommend a simple three-step process called *permission, praise,* and *possibilities.*

Here is a recent example:
Kari, a 36-year-old former emergency room trauma nurse, has changed her career path. She's currently employed at a nonprofit organization that raises funds to offer medical aid and services to refugees around the world. Before this job, Kari was in a setting where commands and strict control were the norm. Reprimands, shouting, and negative feedback from authority figures were frequent occurrences. In her previous workplace, abusive behavior was accepted and justified due to the urgent nature of the work involving life-and-death situations.

In her new role, Kari was under the supervision of Josh, who lacked medical knowledge and sought out Kari for her trauma experience and decision-making. Josh was frustrated by Kari's reluctance to offer insights, suggestions, or highlight errors.

The first time I met with them, Josh shared an incident where he had accidentally over-ordered a supply of bandages. The bulky boxes occupied valuable space during shipment, ultimately excluding essential items like antibiotics. Kari had noticed the mistake, but she assumed that Josh had a valid reason for ordering the surplus bandages, and therefore, she remained silent. When the missing supplies were needed, the oversight impacted many people in critical need of care.

Kari's assumption backfired, as Josh responded with fury, resorting to shouting—the exact behavior that Kari had hoped to escape.

I suggested Kari and Josh implement *permission, praise,* and *possibilities.*

Permission:
Kari: "Josh, that's a lot of bandages. Can I ask why we're sending so many?"

Praise:
Josh: "I'm really glad you asked. How many do you think we should ship?"

Possibilities:
Josh: "Kari, this is exactly why I chose you for the position. Would it be possible for you to review each order from now on?"

This conversation may seem simplistic, but be assured that there were a LOT of uncomfortable feelings being experienced by both Josh and Kari.

Kari felt timid and afraid of questioning Josh's decisions. Past experiences had conditioned her that questioning authority would only result in harsh reprimands. Kari had internalized the belief that all authority figures held superior knowledge and should not be second-guessed.

On the other side, Josh grappled with bewilderment and confusion. He couldn't understand why a responsible individual wouldn't point out an obvious mistake. Unlike Kari, he hadn't been subjected to harsh treatment before. He wasn't accustomed to praising what he saw as "basic work" but noticed the immediate boost in Kari's confidence. This encouraged him to acknowledge her efforts more frequently. Over the next few months, Josh had to prompt Kari to speak up several times. However, as time went on, her confidence was restored. She began to recognize her value and the trust she held within an engaged and cooperative team.

For those battling Imposter Syndrome, it's essential to recognize it as a learned habit stemming from thoughts, programming, and beliefs fostered by past experiences. I encourage you to begin to pinpoint and challenge these self-sabotaging thoughts consciously. Introducing fresh perspectives like *Permission, Praise, and Possibilities* will create room for new experiences that foster healthy habits.

If you interact with someone facing imposter syndrome, remember that changing habits and patterns takes time. Your empathy, patience, and reassurance are not just beneficial but necessary.

Begin now to shift into observation mode at work. How many conflicts are being caused by those dealing with an imposter mindset? Use the techniques you'll learn in this book to step forward as a model for breaking free from imposter-related limitations. In doing so, you set an example and inspire others to follow suit. Regardless of your title or position, your choices have a ripple effect on others. When you notice yourself or others experiencing Imposter Syndrome, remember that thoughts, patterns, and experiences cause this habit. Be aware of those imposter-perpetuating thoughts and create new ones to combat them. When you create new thoughts, you'll have new experiences, which lead to better habits.

This is just the beginning.

Reflections

Think of a time when you've asked questions of yourself or others that may have been judgmental or based on comparison/competition. What questions or comments can you use next time?

_____
_____
_____
_____
_____

List the names of young women that you care about. Next, write at least three things you admire about them next to their names. Now, instead of imposter-creating topics, you have three positive things to talk about the next time you're together.

_____
_____
_____
_____
_____

REMEMBER:

The best role models for women
are people who are fruitfully
and confidently themselves.

Meryl Streep

2
Conquer Your Imposter

It takes courage to be different, stand up, speak out, and be seen. For many women, the mere thought of visibility triggers the imposter within. The instant she commits to change or taps into her inner courage, the brain often sends a message of danger:

*Enter fear, anxiety, and worries about
what other people think.*

I have seen this happen with hundreds of women, nearly all my clients, and myself.

The very moment we tap into our inner courage, we start to panic and worry about things like:

- Who do I think I am?
- I don't want to appear arrogant, bossy, or make others uncomfortable.
- What will my boss/colleague/partner/mom/ sister/neigh bor say?
- What will my boss/colleague/partner/mom/sister/ neighbor THINK?
- I will get criticized, be judged, and maybe even canceled.
- It's probably smarter and safer to just be quiet, keep my head down, and keep those thoughts to myself.

PLEASE DO NOT let these natural thoughts and fears keep you small or derail your ideas. Understand that this form of sabotage is simply an automatic defense system to keep you safe.

Being courageous and speaking out about outdated beliefs and practices can make others uncomfortable. In my own life, there have been instances when I've spoken to the media, expressed differing opinions from fellow panelists, or shared information that I knew other women supported but hesitated to voice. Each time, I held my breath and feared criticism, only to have people nod in agreement and whisper, "I wish I had your courage."

Challenging long-held beliefs, habits, and practices can feel uncomfortable, but our fears rarely unfold. Like you, when I am about to speak up, I feel tightness in my chest and throat, the panicked feelings when wondering what others will think, say, or do. I still cringe with that familiar sinking feeling when reading an inbox message that begins with, "You don't know me, but..."

GULP.

Yes, it's an uncomfortable feeling, and when the criticism happens, it's not fun. Most of the time, I say what needs to be said because receiving a few critical comments is far less scary than the perpetuation of whatever belief I'm disputing. When I feel afraid and want to hide, here is what I do:

- I remember the times I spoke up, and good came from it.
- I remember the messages from women who con tacted me and thanked me for saying what they were afraid to say, expressing that I gave them the

courage to speak up as well.
- I remember the policies that were adjusted because I dared to suggest changes.
- I remember when I was too afraid to speak up but secretly admired those who were making changes and being bold. They inspired my courage.
- I think of the brave women who came generations before me and dared to foster change that demanded equality.
- I think of my ancestors, the pioneers in my family who hid with their children behind a secret door in the kitchen fireplace to avoid capture during the war.

TAKE INSPIRATION FROM OTHERS

When I think of women in history who stood up for the right to vote, dignity and equality for all, access to quality health care, financial independence, the right to own land, etc., my fears pale in comparison. Making the phone call, sending the email, stating the truth, publishing the book, or asking that reporter for an interview seems insignificant. I find my courage by remembering them.

In my journal, I keep a list of people I admire. When I'm struggling with fear or lack of confidence, I imagine the advice that they would give me. Here are a few who are on my list:

Nelly Bly, who grew up not far from me, became a reporter at age 16. The year was 1885, and she sent a scathing letter to the editor about a news story promoting female infanticide. Her courage to speak out landed her a paying job as a reporter for the same newspaper. She had to write under an assumed name, of course, but over the years, Nelly became world-famous for her groundbreaking global stories. She is credited for exposing inhumane living conditions in asylums for the mentally ill.

Malala Yousafzai is one of the most courageous women I am familiar with. Originally from Pakistan, she was born into a culture that didn't celebrate the birth of girls. Her father was forward-thinking and ran a school for girls. In 2008, when Malala was nine years old, the Taliban took over her village and forbade things like television, music, and education for girls. At the age of 14, she bravely spoke out publicly against the Taliban, demanding educational rights for girls, and became an instant target. One afternoon, a masked gunman boarded the school bus and shot her in the head. She miraculously survived the attempt on her life but became a refugee. She and her parents were resettled in the United Kingdom. After undergoing many surgeries and rehabilitation, she studied philosophy, economics, and politics at the University of Oxford. Today, Malala is a bestselling author, lecturer, and the youngest-ever winner of the Nobel Peace Prize. She remains an activist, working worldwide to fight poverty, promote education, combat gender discrimination, and end child marriage.

Golda Meir arrived in the United States with her family as refugees when she was just eight years old. She recognized the importance of education as a young girl and, at age ten, started an organization to raise money to purchase textbooks for young children. At age 14, Golda's father insisted she drop out of school to be married. She ran away from home and lived with her sister until she was allowed to return to school. She eventually married and also helped establish the country of Israel, later becoming the second and only female Prime Minister.

Mary Kay Ash, the creator of Mary Kay Cosmetics, started her company with her entire retirement savings of $5,000. An iconic leader and victim of employment discrimination, she set out in 1963 to create a company where women would be paid fairly and earn promotions, raises, and incentives based on performance instead of gender. She was ahead of her time all the time. Mary Kay changed the business world by allowing women to control their own futures. She has been a role model to me since I was very young.

Besides famous women from history, I also draw inspiration from the women in my family.

Ann Thompson Oliver, my great-grandmother, came to the United States on a boat from England with her family when she was 12 years old. She married three times, had two children, and had a job, even though, at that time, women needed permission from their husbands to even have a bank account. She did not believe that women should have to put up with violence, adultery, alcoholism, or other "nonsense" from men. She reminded me of this many times when I was growing up. She saved her money, purchased mink coats and diamonds for herself, traveled around the world, did whatever she wanted, and let me know that it was perfectly fine to do the same.

Rachel Caldwell, grandmother of my grandmother's who, in the late 1700s, settled with her husband James in the wilderness of Lancaster County, Pennsylvania. She often hid herself and seven children behind the stone wall of the homestead's fireplace, sometimes for days, to protect them from capture during the Revolutionary War. My grandfather told me the story when I was very young, and I still think of it often, amazed by her courage and fortitude.

I encourage you to create an admiration list of your own. Whenever you are in the process of taking significant action and suddenly lose your courage, take a look at your list. Imagine what advice they would give to you. This is one of my favorite ways to overcome brain fear and take action.

Fear is a natural part of being human. Bear in mind that you are a work-in-progress and improving all the time. The future is filled with unlimited potential and possibilities for you.

Reflections

List five people whom you admire. They can be well-known history-makers, deceased or alive, fictional or related to you. Write what you specifically admire in them and what they did when facing challenges.

_____

_____

_____

_____

_____

What are some accomplishments that you're most proud of? Write a few things here that you can remember when you feel afraid.

_____

_____

_____

_____

_____

What activities make you feel most confident?

_____

_____

_____

_____

_____

Now, let's get onto banishing Imposter Syndrome. Are you ready?

Don't let thoughts and fears keep you
from doing what you were meant to do.
The world is waiting for your gifts.

Beth Caldwell

3
Recognize the Imposter

Imposter Syndrome, like many habits, is one that is deeply embedded in our minds and culture. Changing this habit is not like turning off a light switch. You don't just wake up one day and say, "Oh, hello, Imposter Syndrome, it's you. Now, begone forever."

Banishing the imposter begins with noticing your own individual patterns and habits. It will take a little more than just awareness, but becoming aware of the imposter is the crucial first step in the process.

How do you recognize the imposter? Here are some ways it may appear in your daily life:

- Walking into a room of colleagues or other professionals and feeling that you don't belong.
- Raising your hand to volunteer at work, then pulling it back down immediately as you think to yourself, "Someone else is more qualified."
- Receiving an award or recognition and thinking, "They've made a mistake."
- Receiving an award or recognition, not telling anyone, or not showing up for the celebration.
- Spending excess time reviewing your work because you think it may not be perfect enough.
- Not sharing a thought, idea, or opinion to avoid looking dumb.
- Obsessively and constantly trying to prove your worth and impress those around you.

- Apologizing for having a thought or an idea.
- Worrying that your presence, ideas, or suggestions will make others uncomfortable.
- Beating yourself up for past mistakes.
- Not willing to try something because you made a mistake or didn't do things perfectly the first time.
- Not trusting your intuition.
- Not taking a chance because you imagine or expect the worst possible outcomes.
- Doing other people's work or taking on extra work.
- Dismissing praise.
- Continually seeking certifications, designations, or credibility from external sources.

This imposter is a sinister gremlin, isn't it?

AVOID THE IMPOSTER TRAP

As you read this list, do you find yourself nodding in agreement and thinking of examples from your own life? If so, remember that this is not a time to self-criticize. Learning to recognize the imposter is a process. Here is what I recommend to prevent falling into the imposter's trap.

1. Notice the Pattern

You notice that you've just held back, stayed small, missed an opportunity, or criticized yourself. Maybe it was in your thoughts, a text or email, or perhaps at a work meeting. You catered to others, allowed them to minimize or overlook you, and didn't speak up for yourself, speak the truth, or say what you wanted. The first few times you notice this, try using a pattern interrupter: If appropriate, say aloud, "AHA! HELLO IMPOSTER! I SEE YOU." Resist the urge to say or think something like "I'm so stupid" or "I cannot believe I did that again!" Remember, Imposter Syndrome is a deeply embedded subconscious pattern. You may be so accustomed to this programming that you don't even notice the imposter's appearance at first. Don't give up. Keep observing yourself.

2. Catch the Imposter in the Moment

Once you begin to notice the appearance of the imposter after it occurred, you'll soon start to realize the habit as it's taking place. You may find yourself mid-sentence thinking, "OH, I'm doing it again." That's good. You noticed this pattern while it was taking place. Now say to yourself, "Oh, that's interesting. I had the opportunity to _____, but I avoided it. HMMM." I like to use the word interesting because it's a neutral word with no judgment attached. You are simply stating an observation. This can often happen when sending a written message via email or text, which is ideal because you can use the backspace keys and rewrite your words. When you find yourself in this space, know that progress is occurring.

3. Catch the Imposter Before the it Appears

Once you notice the imposter, as it's happening, very quickly, you'll begin to catch yourself JUST BEFORE that imposter pops up. The first few times can feel awkward, but you are creating a new habit and now get to make a different choice. You might dig in and say, "I volunteer," "Thank you, I appreciate the compliment," or "I'd like to be considered for the position."

It doesn't matter how long it takes to work through the three phases of moving from imposter syndrome to personal freedom. This is not a race or competition. When old patterns and habits, be kind to yourself. This can happen especially when you are under stress, lacking sleep, or in a rush. After some time, you will find that where you once excelled at beating yourself up, you can simply notice what's happened, consider the circumstances, and set intentions to do better next time.

Reflections

When did you first notice the imposter appearing in your daily life?

_____

_____

_____

_____

_____

_____

What ideas, projects, or other pursuits have you put off recently because of imposter syndrome?

_____

_____

_____

_____

_____

_____

If it weren't for your imposter, what are a few things you might try?

_____

_____

_____

_____

_____

_____

We've just learned the first important step in conquering the imposter: **Recognize The Imposter.**

 Recognize The Imposter

Ready for the next step? Read on.

It's not who you are that holds you back.
It's who you think you're not.

Beth Caldwell

4
Remember Your Truth

We were born knowing the truth about our innate abilities and talents. As young children, we believed we could do, be, have, and create what we wished. Then teachers, parents, other adults, and society trained those thoughts right out of us.

Children today are exposed to movies and stories that depict powerful princesses and women who defy stereotypes, but until recently, messages from the media were more limited. There are women in the workforce today who were encouraged to become teachers or nurses, to go into marketing instead of business, and to nursing school instead of medical school. When you were growing up or making a school choice, you may have experienced or heard something like this:

-Math is hard; are you sure you want to try that?
-No one likes a smarty-pants.
-Wouldn't you prefer something less complicated?
-Science in college is more complex than in high
 school.
-Women bosses are bitches.
-Strong girls can be intimidating.

You will come across people who still embrace these ideas, and they may be leading schools, churches, companies, families, and some governments in the world. Even if we KNOW intellectually that these messages are not true, they can be internalized only to resurface later in life. You may struggle with these thoughts when stepping out of your comfort zone, stretching for a big goal, or making those around you uncomfortable.

I've heard endless stories from accomplished women who, in their youth, were discouraged by parents, teachers, and religious leaders, unknowingly planting the seeds of imposter syndrome. Now that we know better, we can remind ourselves and each other to remember our truth.

Like you, I've had experiences that fostered imposter syndrome and have had to remember my truth. By age 11, I was an obsessive reader; my constant companion was a book or magazine. I was inspired by women athletes, writers, and executives and actively imagined myself leading a company (or a country) one day.

My teacher that year, Mrs. Hopper, was a traditional and God-fearing woman who believed girls were meant to be quiet, helpful, and patient. One February afternoon year, she'd had enough of my big ideas. As a punishment for "reading too much," she took my eyeglasses away. She announced to the class that I had done enough reading for a lifetime. I dared not tell my parents about this incident. When my mom asked where my glasses were, I simply said, "They are at school." Mrs. Hopper kept my glasses until the last day of school, then returned them to me with a stern warning: "No one likes a smarty-pants."

While I was excited to be able to read again, I internalized her message. That experience caused me to let go of my fantasies of running an empire one day.

In the school years that followed, I stayed quiet and kept my head down. I never wanted to be called "smarty pants" again.

Throughout the early years of my career, I kept my optimism and spirit but had a very tough experience with a boss. I was working at a dysfunctional company in the airline industry. It was fast-paced and fun, but the leadership was old school. I applied for a manager position that, despite my inexperience, I knew I could do well. On the day of the interview, I dressed in a new suit and got up early to prepare. I remember looking in the mirror that morning and saying, "Tonight, and from now on, everything will be different." My coworkers were impressed by my ambition and cheered me on as I boarded the airplane for the job interview. I took a notebook with me that was filled with ideas and improvements. There was no interview. The company representative told me he'd heard about my nice a$$ and wanted to see it in person. He stifled a laugh before scolding me for wasting company time. I didn't start crying until I got home that evening. I looked in that same mirror and said, "You idiot. You should have known better." Things were different for me beginning that night. I was filled with shame and embarrassment. It was a long time before my natural enthusiasm and optimism returned.

If you had been there with me that evening, you probably wouldn't have called me an idiot. You might have said something like:

• That was really brave.
• He is arrogant.
• That's illegal.

- They lost out.
- I hope you don't give up.
- I hope you try again.
- They would be lucky to have you.
- I am proud of you for trying.

I did not ask for advice from friends that evening. I was humiliated and angry with myself. Those feelings of shame and embarrassment caused me to put in for a transfer immediately, and despite loving my job and co-workers, I was gone within two weeks. I moved to a new city, determined to put the experience in the past. This is when the imposter truly took hold of me. I temporarily lost sight of my truth, and it took years to recover.

When we lose our truth, we start to give up things that bring us joy but cause discomfort in those around us. When the imposter got to me, I stopped listening to music, writing in my journal, dancing with friends, and taking long walks in the park. Instead, I filled my days and nights with attending parties, learning to cook, accepting blind dates, and making choices to make others happy. I slowly became bitter and miserable by keeping others comfortable and happy.

Years later, as I was venting about the circumstances I was tolerating at the time, a brilliant coach, Tom Volkar, gently let me know that I had some deep inner work to do. I'll never forget when he said, "Beth, coping isn't living." It was time for me to remember my truth. Those four words and the realization that followed forever changed the path of my life and career.

It wasn't long before I realized that re-discovering that truth was much easier than avoiding my gifts. This was one of my most important life lessons. In my attempts to put a former teacher and boss at ease, I was with-holding my gifts from the world.

AVOID THE IMPOSTER TRAP

That advice I received from Tom prompted me to heal the inner trauma that initially planted the imposter within me and created this desire to stay small. The common practice is to begin with your earliest traumatic memory. With his guidance, I navigated the following exercise:

1. Face The Feelings

In my mind, I went back in time and revisited the encounter with the teacher who took my glasses. Instead of concealing the emotions, I embraced them fully. The awkwardness, shame, embarrassment, frustration, injustice, panic, worry—-I allowed each sensation to wash over me. It felt profoundly unjust! Although it seemed to take forever, the experience lasted just a few minutes. Subsequently, a sense of sadness and disillusionment settled in, as well as wishing I had the skills back then to better navigate that experience.

2. Revisit The Experience From An Adult Perspective

Next, under the supervision of my coach, I envisioned the teacher confiscating my glasses and directing her stern comments to the adult version of myself.

I imagined myself in a composed manner, communicating to Mrs. Hopper that today's world provides a safe space for girls to embrace their intelligence, creativity, and independence. I envisioned her comprehension, a nod of affirmation, and a swell of pride for my accomplishments. It dawned on me then that her intentions may have stemmed from a wish not to cause harm but perhaps from a desire to be realistic and prevent disappointment.

3. Forgive And Release

Next, my coach informed me that it was time to forgive and release the experience. He explained that I no longer needed the emotions. They had lost their purpose. The lesson was learned, and the memory no longer held value. Though I was reluctant, I agreed to participate in a forgiveness exercise. It was simple. I said aloud, "Mrs. Hopper, I forgive you. All is well." I must admit that part of me expected the window to burst open in a blaze of lightning and wind. That's the sensation when you're disentangling from emotions and patterns that have been nurtured for a very long time. Although nothing dramatic occurred at that moment, I soon noticed a renewed confidence and began participating in activities I had ignored for years. A heightened sense of creativity, happiness, and serenity gradually settled in.

That exercise profoundly affected my life, and it was about half of that one-hour coaching session. Since then, I've repeated this forgiveness exercise many times, including the man who interviewed my a$$.

HOW TO RELEASE YOUR IMPOSTER

1. Face The Feelings

In a safe place, and under the guidance of a mental health practitioner or professional when needed, enter the realm of introspection. In your mind, journey back in time and relive an encounter where someone stole your confidence or caused you to doubt yourself. Instead of shying away from the emotions, embrace them. You may want to journal the feelings.

2. Revisit the Experience from an Adult Perspective

Now, under professional guidance, if necessary, visualize the individual's actions directed at your adult self. How would you respond as a mature, insightful, enlightened, intelligent, and articulate adult? Envision a dialogue where you communicate the results of their actions. Adopting an adult perspective within this scenario allows you to equip the younger version of yourself with the tools she lacked at that time, empowering her to navigate the situation effectively.

3. Forgive and Release

The third step in reconnecting with your authentic self is to forgive those who took that truth from you and release the memory. It's time to let go of that story now and remove the narrative that has been replaying in your subconscious. Recognize that the memory of this experience is not helpful, is not keeping you safe, and you no longer have a use for it. This step may be as uncomfortable as reliving the experience, so take your time. You've likely been carrying this emotional weight for a long time, and it's become an ingrained part of your emotional landscape. Should you feel resistant towards the concept of forgiveness, feel free to revisit steps one and two as often as necessary. When you're ready, you might write a forgiveness mantra in your journal, or say the words aloud, "I forgive you and release this memory," or simply make an internal decision to let the feelings go.

Letting go of past experiences allows us to rediscover who we truly are and remember what we really believed about ourselves before we learned to adapt to make those around us more comfortable. This process of releasing takes time, and there is no set limit. You might go through this exercise for several different experiences. Since we all have unique life stories, some people may need to enlist the help of a therapist, mental health, holistic energy practitioner, or life coach.

Reflections

What experiences occurred in your youth that planted the seeds of imposter syndrome?

_____

_____

_____

_____

_____

_____

Imagine visiting your young self before you were ten years old. What were her dreams? What activities have you stopped doing that she enjoyed?

_____

_____

_____

_____

_____

_____

Who do you need to forgive for seeding imposter syndrome in your life?

_____

_____

_____

_____

_____

_____

What stories have you been telling yourself and hanging on to?

_____

_____

_____

_____

What stories are you ready to let go of, beginning today?

_____

_____

_____

You've just learned step two of overcoming the imposter: **Recognize The Imposter.**

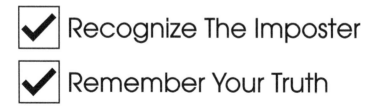

☑ Recognize The Imposter

☑ Remember Your Truth

Let's dive into step three.

Your inner voice will never lie to you.

Beth Caldwell

5
Trust Your Inner Voice

Intuition is a gift. It's the sixth sense that will always lead us in the right direction. We've been trained to be obedient and ignore the inner promptings of our minds, which is very sad.

Your intuition is the ability to know or feel something without proof. Your inner voice can always be trusted. It will never lie to you, so honor it, especially when it's providing a warning. Prior to the patriarchy, women's intuition was highly regarded, and it's becoming acceptable again. Men and women are becoming more comfortable using and trusting their inner voice.

Have you ever had a hunch, feeling, or intuition that you ignored? Have you ever regretted it? Perhaps a job you didn't want to take but accepted it anyway? Maybe you hired someone who didn't feel like a good fit? Or dated someone who your gut told you wasn't suitable for you?

We've been taught to listen to external opinions and ignore our personal feelings. I see women in my coaching practice who spend months and years putting off their desires because they have been programmed to please. They have an idea and instantly think of why they should not do it or how they will fail. They have been trained to ignore their intuition.

Have you noticed that women often feel dissatisfied with their lives, careers, or relationships yet hesitate to make changes? They long to do and be something different, yet they hold back because they don't want to be criticized or disappoint others.

If you're feeling dissatisfied and yearning for something different, recognize that your inner voice is trying to communicate! If you keep ignoring those promptings, you'll become more unhappy and may eventually become bitter, resentful, and miserable.

One thing I've noticed about dissatisfied women is that they continually "should" themselves. Do these comments seem familiar to you?

- You should be more organized.
- You should exercise more.
- You should lose weight.
- You should volunteer more.
- You should not complain.
- You should not boast.
- You should not feel sad.
- You should eat more vegetables.
- You should drink more water.
- You should do more.
- You should give more.
- You should apologize.
- You should be ashamed.
- You should be grateful.
- You should be happy with what you have.

How often have you been "should-ed" by yourself or others this week?

"Should-ing" feeds the imposter and negates our intuition. It fosters feelings of guilt, shame, and obligation in young girls and creates adult women who feel it's their responsibility to be non-disruptive and keep everyone happy. These messages are programmed into us by families, teachers, religious institutions, authority figures, and the media.

When you notice these thoughts, recognize that they have been created by an external agenda, usually for the benefit of others, and not your inner guidance system.

Clinical research studies show that intuition can be faster than reflection and more accurate.

How do you feel about trusting your intuition when making important decisions at home or work? If you're unsure, you're not alone. We've been taught to believe that making decisions without relying on facts is risky, but do we rely too much on facts? The US Office of Naval Research believes in the potential of intuition. They recently conducted studies to help marines and sailors learn to use gut instincts to have an extra edge in decision-making when faced with life-threatening situations. In research studies, women are shown to be naturally intuitive and more in touch with life-saving instincts. Keep that in mind if you are doubting yourself.

Here are some of my favorite examples of intuition-based decision-making:

- **Oprah Winfrey** trusted what she calls her still, small inner voice when moving to Chicago to take a new job, even though her boss warned that it would be the end of her career. She became one of the biggest media influencers of the century and a multi-billionaire. Oprah has been recognized as the greatest Black philanthropist in American history and the most influential woman in the world. She credits her intuition for the most important choices in her life.

- At 16, **Joan of Arc** displayed exceptional trust in her inner voice. In 1428, it was acceptable for a peasant family to arrange marriages for their children. Joan took the unconventional step of challenging her father's arranged marriage and took him to court. She represented herself, and remarkably, she emerged victorious. Less than a year later, Joan went on to lead her country into battle; three years later, she became the revered national heroine of her fellow compatriots. Her remarkable achievements played a pivotal role in the later awakening of French national consciousness.

- **Estée Lauder** disrupted the cosmetics industry in the early 1950s with her successful marketing techniques. The all-male industry dismissed her ideas of giving lipstick color names like Duchess, Crimson, All-Day Rose, and Dancing Red. They mocked her ideas of using pretty packages for cosmetics and warned her that she'd go bankrupt by offering free samples and gift-with-purchase promotions. Esteé persisted. She knew what women liked and was certain her ideas would boost sales. She was right. That year, Estée became the wealthiest self-made woman in the world.

- When **Indra Nooyi** took on the role of CEO at PepsiCo, she broke barriers as the first woman of color and immigrant to head a Fortune 50 company. She broke the pattern of her predecessors, who focused solely on immediate profits. Indra and her husband had two daughters, and she knew that families were seeking healthier choices in grocery aisles. Charting a course for long-term success, Indra pursued a health-focused vision for PepsiCo. She faced brutal criticism. Analysts ridiculed her attempts to make convenience food healthier, even sarcastically calling her "Mother Teresa." Nevertheless, Indra spearheaded successful acquisitions of companies like Quaker Oats, Gatorade, and Tropicana as part of her plan to provide healthier options for today's families. Her path to success was challenging, but her commitment to a long-term strategy paid off. The company's revenue has consistently surpassed expectations, proving the effectiveness of her approach.

LEARNING TO TRUST YOURSELF AGAIN

Have you ever found yourself being ridiculed, mocked, or bullied for having ideas that are different, for sharing your feelings, or for being yourself? When that happens, we can begin to go outside of ourselves for approval. It's natural to want to be liked and accepted. Still, the moment you stop trusting yourself and making decisions based on other peoples' desires and a need for approval, you'll slip down the imposter slope again, leading to feelings of bitterness, resentment, and dissatisfaction. If you are feeling that way, chances are you're trying to please others and ignoring your inner voice. It's tough to trust yourself when constantly listening to the opinions of others, so be sure to insulate yourself against this.

Here are some strategies that can help you to get back in touch with your inner voice, trust your inner guidance, and stop "should-ing" pleasing and avoiding.

1. Get in the habit of being in a quiet environment

It's tough for your inner voice to speak to you when constantly surrounded by noise. Try being silent for just a few minutes each day. Begin with some quiet time in the mornings, evenings, and while driving. If you go for a walk, go without headphones. Silence will be uncomfortable if you're used to constant noise, but hold out. Once you get in the habit of a few silent minutes, use the silence to ask important questions. What is a good solution for ____? What do I really want? What would it take for me to be able to ____? What do I want to stop doing?

2. Use the 5-4-3-2-1 technique to quiet your mind

Usually recommended for anxiety, this technique will help slow thinking and relax your mind. Take a few deep breaths and name five things you can see, four things you can touch, three things you can hear, two things you can smell, and one thing you can taste.

3. Pay attention to your thoughts and dreams

When you are having silent moments, notice the thoughts that pop into your mind. Instead of judging, take notice. Are there patterns? Is your inner voice trying to communicate? When you first wake up in the morning, be still and recall your dreams. Write your thoughts and dreams in a journal and see if you notice any patterns. Be curious. Is your subconscious trying to tell you something?

4. Use Guided Meditations

I do this several times a week. You can find options in most bookstores, many apps, and online. I personally enjoy MindValley mediations. Anytime you meditate, whether on your own or under guidance, have a pen and journal to note any thoughts, patterns, and messages.

5. Spend quiet time in nature

Sometimes, this only happens if it is scheduled in advance. What are some places in nature that you've wanted to visit but haven't yet? Hiking trails, parks, lakes, waterfalls, beaches, mountains, forests, etc.? They can be in your community or anywhere in the world. Make a list. Then, schedule those visits into your calendar.

6. Act on your inner guidance

When you get a prompting, take action. As you begin to experience positive results, the trust grows, and the actions become easier.

7. Seek a friend, coach, support group, or professional for guidance

Be sure that the person you trust to help you has a life, career, and relationships you admire. If they don't, keep looking. You do not have to settle, be "should-ed," or should yourself ever again.

You might be curious about how these seven strategies will be beneficial. Once you set aside time and create a space to listen to your inner thoughts, you'll begin to recognize that some of the thoughts and ideas you've absorbed aren't really helpful for you. You'll find it easier to let go of those persistent thoughts as time passes.

Learning to trust your inner voice will take time and practice for some. Being a "should-er" is a habit you've nurtured, and patterns can be changed. Making life changes takes courage and resilience, so keep at it. I'd rather you feel nervous and uncertain for a little while than bitter and resentful for the rest of your life.

Reflections

How would life be different for all of us if women like Estée Lauder, Oprah Winfrey, Joan of Arc, Indra Nooyi, and so many others backed down to the opinions of others?

_____
_____
_____
_____
_____

What would happen if more of us shared the courage of these women?

_____
_____
_____
_____
_____

What would life be like if you trusted yourself to make decisions based on what is best for your situation instead of what would make others happy?

_____
_____
_____
_____
_____

You've just learned step three in overcoming the imposter: **Trust Your Inner Voice.**

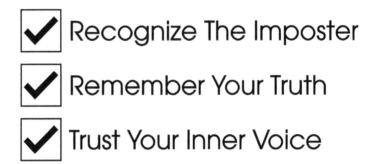

☑ Recognize The Imposter

☑ Remember Your Truth

☑ Trust Your Inner Voice

Learning to trust that voice will be very helpful in mastering the next step. Let's discover step four now.

Facing the truth takes the power
away from the imposter.

Beth Caldwell

6
Take Full Responsibility

Another sneaky way that the imposter gets us is by making it easy to use excuses. We've been programmed to think like this:

"I am very unhappy in my job, but my family depends on my income, so I must accept things as they are."

What if we shifted that thought to:

"The truth is, my family depends on my income, and this job is toxic. It's time to find another income source that aligns with my values. It's important that I am happy and my work is fulfilling."

Telling the truth allows us to accept responsibility, which isn't always easy. Sometimes, we feel embarrassed or ashamed because we've made excuses to avoid conflict. This is especially true in personal relationships and other situations where you may have tolerated unhappy circumstances for many months or years.

Why do we avoid telling the truth? The answer is simple. We don't want to experience pain, awkwardness, or other uncomfortable emotions. We don't want to disappoint or let anyone down, so we continue to live out lies that make us frustrated or unhappy. Everyone does it, and it happens at work and at home.

I began experimenting with telling the truth to myself

and others after learning about emotional response times in the book **Whole Brain Living** by neuroanatomist Dr. Jill Bolte Taylor. This book shares Dr. Taylor's research on emotions, proof that it takes our brains between 5 and 90 seconds to process an emotion fully. So, for example, if you're annoyed that the dry cleaner is not open when you stop by, that emotion should be processed in 5-10 seconds. Something more serious, even as tragic as a betrayal or significant loss, can be fully processed in 90 seconds. Anything after that is a choice. Dr. Jill says that if you're feeling emotions or staying angry for more than 90 seconds, you're giving up personal freedom. I found this research fascinating and immediately began tracking tough emotions. My experiences lined up exactly like her test subjects, ranging from 5 to 90 seconds, and I bet yours will also. When you grasp this concept, telling the truth and facing conflict shift from fearful, dramatic, and avoid-at-all-costs to no-big-deal adjustments.

Two essential things to know about telling the truth, no matter how dire the circumstances:

1. When a person hears upsetting news for the first time, the initial emotional response lasts between 5 and 90 seconds.
2. Once the truth is exposed, the brain will begin to seek solutions immediately.

Here are some truth-in-the-workplace examples:

A medical research company had an employee who stubbornly refused to learn their newest software program. This employee had the reputation of having a temper. His manager and the HR director, both female, had tried to enroll him in training programs for several years without success. Eventually, other employees became frustrated with picking up the slack for him not doing his work and moved to other companies. We scheduled a meeting to discuss options. They were very intimidated and wanted to avoid confrontation. When I told them the only solution was telling the truth, they begged me to do it for them. Here is how that conversation went:

"John, you don't seem to be happy with the new software. The truth is, you'll have to learn either how to use this program and do your job or find another position either in this company or another."

This statement was followed by about 15 seconds of awkward silence. John shifted in his seat and replied, "I didn't know I could move to another department. I would be very happy working in security and prefer to work the night shift."

Beginning to end, the "confrontation" was less than five minutes. All three participants were astonished at how easy it was. Had someone taken responsibility sooner, so much time would have been saved. This team spent years feeling frustrated and avoiding the conflict. That very week, they spent days worrying about how that conversation would go, imagining the worst. In that case, telling the truth turned out to be emotionally easier than avoiding it. Taking responsibility saves time, money, and anguish.

Another workplace client had the unfortunate task of choosing seven people to let go. This mortgage processing company was like a little family with 35 employees. Choosing seven seemed impossible to the regional president. He had already delayed facing this decision for six months, and the company was now experiencing significant financial hardship. He hired me to help assess the situation. It was my job to help him take responsibility and make the decisions.

I visited once a week for six weeks, getting to know the people and their roles. The truth was the company was over-staffed. The excess workforce led to lots of idle time among the employees. The president did not seem to notice this, as he was in emotional distress. He was obsessed with the employee's personal situations and found it impossible to be objective. He knew who had student loans, who had children, and who just financed a new home.

After five difficult weeks of deliberation, seven employees were chosen to be eliminated. We dreaded the conversations that awaited us the following Friday. I was more removed than he, but it was still upsetting. Before 10:00 a.m. that day, we repeated the same line seven times, "We regret to inform you that your position has been eliminated due to recent restructuring efforts within the company. Today is your last day of employment." We went through a lot of tissues, gave a lot of long hugs, and debriefed when it was over.

We found the conversations easier than expected and observed a pattern among those being let go.

Surprisingly, many acknowledged their sadness about departing yet confessed they hadn't particularly enjoyed their time at the company. One employee expressed relief as she now had a genuine motive to relocate closer to her family. While a few were clearly shaken and anxious, I, being emotionally detached from the situation, was able to observe a consistent pattern. In each instance, the raw emotions—such as shock, sadness, surprise, uncertainty, and defensiveness— lasted only about 30 seconds. Yet, as they mentally processed the situation, a rapid shift occurred. The focus transitioned from these intense emotions to pragmatic and action-oriented questions. The inquiries ranged from asking about severance packages to unemployment benefits and health insurance concerns. Some even began contemplating new directions, wondering if returning to school was a possibility and even suggesting that other companies were hiring in the region.

The regional president realized that by avoiding conflict for more than six months, he'd been responsible for draining funds and had limited the options for the people he cared about. If you've found yourself in a similar situation, remember that these tough lessons help us become more effective leaders. I know it's been much easier for me to face conflict since that experience. That regional president is now a national president. He now faces conflict without hesitation. He learned from experience that taking responsibility sooner rather than later is best.

What conversations have you been avoiding at work and home to simply spare yourself from confrontation, conflict, or experiencing the emotions of others? Have you ever said "that's okay" when you really wanted to say "that's disappointing"?

Me too. In fact, that was the first truth I admitted to myself. Not long ago, my partner constantly changed our weekend plans because his college-age child would ask for a ride at the last minute. At first, I said, "That's okay. I have plenty to do to keep busy." Then, when I finally got frustrated and annoyed enough, I responded, "I'm disappointed."

I'll never forget the look on his face that morning. He was shocked and couldn't speak for a moment. He remarked that he didn't think the changes in plans bothered me at all. (Of course, he didn't because I kept telling him it was fine!) When he realized that the last-minute changes frustrated me, he admitted that they frustrated him too. That evening, he requested a few day's notice from now on and received an apology. After that, plans were made a week in advance, or other rides were arranged. This didn't happen until I stopped making excuses for others, stopped pretending I was okay, and, instead of expecting him to notice my disappointment, took responsibility for expressing my feelings.

Telling the truth can be easier than keeping frustrations and disappointments to yourself. The first place you can begin telling the truth is with yourself. Here are some truths that I've learned to admit to myself over the years:

I am taking good care of everyone but me.
This workplace is toxic.
This relationship is not healthy for me.
I am living in reactive mode.
I'm procrastinating because of a fear of criticism.
I'm procrastinating because of a fear of success.

Taking on projects that keep me busy is a form of procrastination
I have dreams but resist them because people will make fun of me.

Do any of these truths resonate with you? You are not alone! It feels frustrating to realize that we have created these situations, but please be compassionate with yourself. I remind my clients often that "beating yourself up gives you nothing but bruises."

Admitting the truth of a situation allows us to take full responsibility and get back on course. The imposter can be sneaky and tell you that your assertion will disappoint others, hurt their feelings, or make them feel uncomfortable. Remind yourself that the truth opens the way for solutions, and your happiness is your responsibility.

PERSONAL RESPONSIBILITY STATEMENT

If you have been avoiding emotions, staying clear of conflict, and doing your best to keep the peace by not complaining, here is a statement that you can use to help ease the feelings of guilt or shame:

The truth is that I avoided admitting _____ because I feared _____ and didn't want to face_____. Admitting this takes courage. I'm ready to take responsibility now.

Facing the truth and claiming responsibility will always take the power away from the imposter.

Reflections

What truths have you been avoiding?

_____

_____

_____

_____

_____

_____

What has been the cost of avoidance?

_____

_____

_____

_____

_____

_____

How can you take steps to move forward?

_____

_____

_____

_____

_____

_____

How can you show more compassion to yourself?

_____
_____
_____
_____
_____
_____
_____

Identify 3-5 people or professionals that can help you
with this new truth.

_____
_____
_____
_____
_____
_____
_____

You just learned step four to overcome the imposter: **Take Full Responsibility.** Facing the truth is one of the most challenging habits to change, but remember, the truth will always take the power away from the imposter.

✓ Recognize The Imposter

✓ Remember Your Truth

✓ Trust Your Inner Voice

✓ Take Full Responsibility

The next strategy is not nearly as hard to learn or implement. Are you ready? Let's discover step five.

Belonging doesn't require us to change who we are, It requires us to be who we are.

Brené Brown

7
Create a Circle of Support

When you are surrounded by people who fill you with support and respect instead of those who criticize and judge you, the imposter loses all of its power.

One of the things I've noticed about women with Imposter Syndrome is that they spend a lot of time surrounded by people who constantly question and criticize their motives. As you begin to embrace the strategies of trusting your inner voice, telling the truth, embracing conflict, and taking responsibility, you might get questioned and criticized. Don't let that surprise you.

If you've noticed that your newly found confidence is making others uncomfortable, CONGRATULATIONS! You're growing. Instead of feeling discouraged or frustrated, remind yourself that everyone is on their own path. Your path may be splitting off a bit. These new habits you've been embracing will have you feeling free and confident, but those around you may still struggle with their own imposter. You don't have to abandon old friends, but allow space to create new, more empowering friendships.

As I navigated my own self-improvement journey, it wasn't easy to accept that not everyone was thrilled with my personal growth. My self-esteem had never been stronger, yet I still wanted to please everyone.

I remember one very critical email that stung so badly that I left the office. Choking back tears, I asked my sweetheart to meet me for a walk. He could tell I was really upset, and we decided to meet at a local hiking trail. I vented. I repeated the contents of the email over and over again. He stopped me on the path, turned me to face him, held my face in his hands, and said, "Hon, have you ever noticed that these people who criticize you are also deeply unhappy individuals?"

Time to tell the truth again. My improvements had made others uncomfortable. They weren't pleased about my success. These recent critics were also some of the unhappiest people I knew. They were living in unhappy marriages, working at jobs they didn't like, and my changes only amplified their unhappiness. They would be much more comfortable if I changed back and be just like them. "Time to find some new friends," I said out loud. That is when I decided to create a new circle of support.

I began considering places to meet like-minded friends who shared my interests. Surrounding myself with positivity was essential, particularly connecting with independent women. My goal was to discover individuals who enjoyed personal development, exploring different cultures, entrepreneurship, and who had a similar passion for reading, writing, attending lectures, and world travel. That year, I joined a speaker's association and two women's leadership groups. Within these groups, I was delighted to discover that my ideas and aspirations were not uncommon at all.

Today, I'm pleased to say that I have several close friends whose lives I both admire and respect. We embrace and praise each other for being nontraditional and cheer on all new adventures. Like me, my new friends sometimes make other people uncomfortable and occasionally still receive criticism, but we have each other to talk things over with. For me, one way to defeat the imposter is to ONLY take advice from people I would gladly trade places with. If they have a life, career, and relationship I respect and admire, their advice is valid and worth listening to. Guess what? My new friends give advice only when I ask!

Who are your champions?

CREATE A CIRCLE OF SUPPORT

Creating a circle of friends who support, admire, and believe in you is possible. Here are some ways that I started my own circle of support:

1. **Gently separate from people and things that make you feel negative.** Instead, fill your calendar with people and events that make you feel content and confident.

2. **List the things you genuinely enjoy and haven't done for a while.** For me, this is reading, writing, learning, traveling, philanthropy, and socializing with like-minded friends.

3. **Look for groups to join.** Join and become active with groups and associations that center around things that interest you. Fans have started book clubs around a particular author. There are groups doing

art and writing projects together at libraries and coffee shops. I enjoy going to story clubs in my hometown each month. My son started a city hiking group recently, and he was surprised to have more than ten people join his first hike. If there is not a group centered around your favorite activity, be bold and start one up. I am certain you can find others who share your interest.

4. **Take classes and courses.** Lifelong learning is a great way to make new friends. There are classes on almost any topic you can imagine, filled with people who also enjoy learning. Try something new... a musical instrument, software design, car repair, cooking, a new language, home remodeling, dance, exercise, etc. Be bold and introduce yourself to others in the class. Invite people to coffee, lunch, walks, or virtual meetings.

5. **Schedule regular get-togethers with friends.** Pre-scheduling dates with friends is very helpful to keep time from slipping by. Creating a recurring event with your friends keeps you engaged and helps to prevent loneliness and isolation. Checking in frequently allows you the time and space to share what's happening in each other's lives.

6. **Start or join a mentoring group at work.** The work place can be lonely, and it's a place where imposter syndrome thrives. A workplace mentoring group is an ideal way to partner with or lead women who find the support of other women helpful.

Spending more time in groups where you can have

fun with people and enjoy experiences that make you feel confident can help to eliminate the imposter once and for all. You don't have to eliminate others from your life; in fact, your renewed confidence and spirit will show them what's possible.

Reflections

What are some activities you've always wanted to do but never tried?

_____

_____

_____

_____

_____

_____

Which community groups or classes can you participate in to potentially meet people with similar interests?

_____

_____

_____

_____

_____

Is there a mentorship group at your workplace or a women's leadership group in your hometown? Make a list of groups or ideas here:

_____

_____

_____

_____

_____

_____

You've just learned step five to overcome the imposter: **Create a Circle of Support.**

☑ Recognize The Imposter

☑ Remember Your Truth

☑ Trust Your Inner Voice

☑ Take Full Responsibility

☑ Create a Circle of Support

Let's move on to the final step in overcoming the imposter.

Don't tell them who you are.
Show them.

Beth Caldwell

8
Show Others the Way

This is a unique time in the evolution of humans, and you're a part of it. Imagine our grandmothers and their grandmothers being able to visit us today and witness this unique time in the evolution of humankind. The imposter has thrived in a society that has, until now, accepted patriarchal beliefs. The world today is experiencing a shift in collective consciousness. We find ourselves positioned at a societal awakening. We're becoming more aware of being interconnected and the need for positive change.

Women often think they need a title to be a leader. In truth, actions, not titles, influence change. So far, you've learned five steps to conquer the imposter. As you implement them, your efforts will show others around you what is possible. How you handle fear, conflict, or even compliments is noticed by those around you, and not just at work. Like it or not, people notice when we do things well or poorly. The ones who stay quiet or never change simply don't get noticed, but YOU are officially a role model and an influencer at work, at home, and in the community.

Generational habits take courage to change. When institutions of power feel threatened, it's not unusual to experience a backlash of fear, anger, and oppression. If you feel uncomfortable being a role model, leader, or influencer during this time of awakening and transition, that's very understandable. Good news, though—you don't have to march, picket, or protest to influence change today.

Don't tell them who you are; show them!

Our Choices Influence the Women of Tomorrow

ELIMINATE FUTURE IMPOSTER SYNDROME

Below is a collection of straightforward, pragmatic approaches to help diminish imposter syndrome. They may push you slightly beyond your comfort zone and may be different than what you're used to. While they may seem uncomfortable or odd, these tools can reduce and perhaps eliminate imposter syndrome altogether.

1. **Get to know someone before you judge them.** I'm so grateful to have been introduced to mindfulness. I used to be quick to judge and held everyone, including myself, to ridiculously high standards. Through mindfulness, I've discovered that disagreeable behaviors often stem from programming or fear. Remember that most people are doing the best they can. If you're fault-finding, try and get to know a person. Really listen to their story to see the situation from a completely different and compassionate perspective. Instead of judging situations, you may find yourself embracing acceptance, compassion, empathy, and understanding.

2. **Trust yourself.** Even when stepping out of your comfort zone, recognize that you are a work in progress, and change takes a lot of courage. If you feel self-critical or doubtful, ask yourself, "If my friend were in this situation, would I be so hard on her?".

3. **Acknowledge yourself.** When you receive recognition, an award, a raise or promotion, get a new client, or do something brave, please pause and acknowledge the achievement. Too often, we rush on to the next project without saying, "WOW, that was good." You may have been taught to believe these thoughts are bragging or boastful, but recognizing your achievements allows you to see how far you have come.
Yes, you will always have more to do, but you don't have to do it all today.

4. **Help to reframe societal pressures.** You may notice yourself or someone else asking a young girl a

question like, "Do you have a boyfriend yet?" or something similar. This is a time to notice, not judge. Anti-imposter does not mean anti-marriage. When this happens, catch it and then ask a follow-up question. Ask something about her. One of my favorites is, "What I really want to know is this: what was the best part of your day today?"

5. **Embrace your strengths and show others how to do the same.** When you catch yourself fixating on areas of weakness, remember that we're not meant to excel at everything. It's perfectly normal not to be proficient at every skill needed in life. Channel your energy towards enhancing strengths. That is where your greatest potential lies. Our uniqueness enriches the world and allows us to complement and support each other in various ways.

6. **Recognize others for their accomplishments.** Do you ever notice people making impressive achievements but keep thoughts to yourself? When you notice a person making a positive change, receiving an award, creating or starting something new, getting published, getting promoted, etc., don't just think, "That's nice." SAY SOMETHING. Your words of encouragement make a difference. Let them know with a pat on the back, a text message, a phone call, or a social media post that you're proud of them and admire their courage. It makes a difference. And guess what? When others see you congratulating and complimenting, they'll do the same. There you go, influencing again.

7. **Create a stop-doing list.** The next time you are writing yourself a long to-do list, create a new

STOP-DOING list. Add to it all the behaviors and activities you're ready to let go of. Give others around you permission to do the same.

8. **Embrace your inner wisdom.** In my twenties, I wanted to be Wonder Woman. In my thirties, I learned that being a wise woman is the complete opposite of being a Wonder Woman. Wonder Woman flies all over the planet, rescuing others. Wise women save themselves first, then shine right where they are all day long. A wise woman doesn't rush to rescue. Instead, she inspires, encourages, and supports those around her, empowering them to save themselves.

9. **Talk about Imposter Syndrome and suggest work place training programs.** Attend book clubs, community discussion groups, and women's leadership gatherings, or host your own solution-focused discussion group with a diverse group of leaders. It's good to hear and learn from the experiences of others.

Remember, the actions we take today are creating a path for the women and leaders of tomorrow.

Reflections

Think of the young women or girls whose growth and happiness are important to you. List their names here:

_____

_____

_____

_____

_____

_____

_____

How can you support the women/girls on this list?

- [ ] Role model
- [ ] Confidant
- [ ] Mentor
- [ ] Study-Buddy
- [ ] Job Shadowing
- [ ] Shopping Partner
- [ ] Sports Events
- [ ] Activities
- [ ] _____
- [ ] _____
- [ ] _____
- [ ] _____

Does your workplace have a mentoring program, a recognition program, or offer workplace training? If so, how can you get involved? If not, how can you get one started?

_____

_____

_____

You've just discovered the sixth and final step to overcoming imposter syndrome. **Now, Pass It On.**

☑ Recognize The Imposter

☑ Remember Your Truth

☑ Trust Your Inner Voice

☑ Take Full Responsibility

☑ Create a Circle of Support

☑ Pass it on

That imposter doesn't seem nearly as scary now, does it?

Let me tell you a story.
She makes it.
The End.

Beth Caldwell

9

Happily Ever After

Now that you know six ways to overcome Imposter Syndrome, it's time to create your own imposter-free life.

You no longer need to run around feeling scattered, exhausted, and disappointed.

You've been taught to seek "happily ever after" by finding a prince, getting married, and doing your best to hit the significant milestones, 20 years, 30 years, 50 years of blissful togetherness. You've been striving to have perfect children and live in happy, perfect homes. You've been taught to get a degree from a good school and get a job in a good industry with a solid company that offers a retirement plan and benefits. If you live in America, you've been watching movies and reading books that end in happily ever after. And now that you've done all they told you to do, you may find yourself not very happy at all.

The people who taught you this did it because they want you to enjoy a safe, respected, secure existence. Why? Because your being secure makes them happy. If you feel you were misled, realize it was not intentional.

Now that you're here and know better, it's time to discover your own path to happiness. You'll find that you'll be more content in your relationships, as a parent, and at work when you seek fulfillment from within yourself rather than relying solely on relationships or your job to prove your worth. I encourage you to continue to learn about yourself and rediscover your inner child. Begin adding activities and people to your life that make you feel alive and happy. Instead of making d ecisions to please others, make decisions that please you. Trust yourself. Do the things that you've put off. It's never too late to begin.

First, you understand, then you forgive, then you get back on the right path. I can't wait to see what you create for yourself.

This **or** That
Life Choices

Unfulfilled	Content
Resentment	Authenticity
Frustration	Wisdom
Bitterness	Gratitude
Competition	Appreciation
Comparison	Acceptance

#bethtoldme

When you are surrounded by people who
fill you with support and respect
instead of those who criticize, mock,
and judge you,
the imposter loses all of its power.

Beth Caldwell

10

Resources

You now have the awareness and strategies to overcome Imposter Syndrome.
I hope this book has equipped and inspired you to eliminate your imposter. The resources and suggestions that follow keep me motivated. I hope they will do the same for you.

To Read

A beneficial book for navigating emotions and overcoming is Whole Brain Living by Jill Bolte Taylor. This fascinating book lends neuroanatomy with psychology to show how we can short-circuit emotional reactivity and find our way to peace.

I Am Malala: How One Girl Stood Up for Education and Changed the World is the bestselling memoir by Nobel Peace Prize winner Malala Yousafzai. It is available for young readers, a children's edition, and a great book to read with your mentor/mentee. It's riveting and profoundly inspirational.

Speaking While Female: 75 Extraordinary Speeches by American Women by Dana Rubin is a book that has me inspired and informed. Dana has uncovered some amazing women from American History. I want to buy this book and give it to every woman I care about. This collection of speeches is the first anthology to spotlight American women speakers from 1637 to the present and explain how each contributed to the nation's making.

To Visit Online

The National Women's History Museum is an innovative online museum dedicated to uncovering, interpreting, and celebrating women's diverse contributions to society. The NWHM fills in significant omissions of women in history books and K-12 education, providing scholarly content and educational programming for teachers, students, and parents. Discover "her-story" here:
www.womenshistory.org

The Malala Fund was founded in 2012 by Malala and Ziauddin Yousafzai. The father/daughter mission is to champion every girl's right to 12 years of free, safe, quality education. Read her full story and keep up with her important work here:
malala.org/malalas-story

Mindbodygreen is an online resource dedicated to helping women live their best lives mentally, physically, spiritually, and emotionally. Here, you'll find a 360-degree approach that weaves together the mental, physical, spiritual, emotional, and environmental aspects of well-being. Check it out at mindbodygreen.com.

A Mighty Girl is the world's most extensive collection of books, toys, movies, and music for parents, teachers, and others dedicated to raising smart, confident, and courageous girls and, of course, for girls themselves! Take a look at amightygirl.com.

The **BethToldMe** Blog is filled with inspiration and motivation. Access this anytime you need some

Vitamin Beth.
Visit www.coachbethcaldwell.com/beth-told-me.

Good Listens

The *Advice for Life with Lynn* podcast is one of my favorites. Lynn Martinez, a TV personality from South Florida, says she started therapy 20 years ago to learn how to fix everyone else. She discovered that we can only fix ourselves. Her tips are authentic, relevant, and inspiring. Subscribe in your favorite podcast app or online at adviceforlifewithlynn.com.

Wickedly Smart Women with Anjel B. Hartwell is a podcast that inspires me every week. Featuring the world's most impressive emerging and established Wickedly Smart Women, this show spotlights, celebrates, and elevates Wickedly Smart Women who are making a massive difference in the world!

Mentorship Programs

Ten Thousand Coffees offers inclusive corporate mentoring programs that help employees grow their networks, feel connected, and launch their careers. www.tenthousandcoffees.com.

Together, a cloud-based mentorship management solution. It helps businesses automate the mentorship program workflow, including registration, scheduling meetings, progress tracking, and reporting. www.TogetherPlatform.com

Since 1904, **Big Brothers Big Sisters** has operated under the belief that inherent in every child is incredible potential. As the nation's largest donor- and volunteer-supported mentoring network, Big Brothers Big Sisters makes meaningful, monitored matches between adult volunteers ("Bigs") and children ("Littles"), ages 5 through young adulthood in communities across the country. Bigs and Littles hang out 2-3 times a month for a few hours doing normal, everyday activities, like seeing a movie, doing homework, playing games, going out to eat, or just hanging out!

Become a mentor and change a child's future for the better. Sign up here: www.bbbs.org/get-involved/become-a-big.

If you are a parent and want to start your child down a path to an even brighter, more promising future, start here: www.bbbs.org/enroll-a-child.

Workplace Training

Overcoming Imposter Syndrome is available as a workplace training and can be delivered in-person or virtually. Other training programs from Beth Caldwell include:

- Intentional Leadership
- Emotional Resilience
- Make Your Brand Statement
- Leadership Academy for Women

Learn more at: www.coachbethcaldwell.com/corporate-training

Meet Your Coach

Beth Caldwell is a self-help author from the United States. She has been helping women make it in a man's world since she was a Girl Scout. You may recognize her from her edgy leadership columns in the *American City Business Journals, ThriveGlobal, Smart Business, or the popular webTV show The Morning Mastermind.*

Beth is well known as the creator of the SHIFT Coaching Program, Leadership Academy, and Success Circle for Women.

She has received several awards, including a *Radical Leadership award, Top 20 Most Influential Women on LinkedIn, 40 Under 40, and The Woman of Courage award.* Her favorite thing to do is help women create the life, love, and business they've always dreamed of. **Overcoming Imposter Syndrome** is her thirteenth book.

Trust yourself.
Do the things that you've put off.
It's never too late to begin.

Beth Caldwell

Other Books from Beth Caldwell

The YES Journal

Women, LEAD! Influential & Effective Strategies for Women Who Lead at Work, at Home, and in the Community

From Frantic to Focused: How to Shift Your Life from Out-of-Control to Streamlined and Successful

Smart Leadership: 12 Simple Strategies to Help You Shift From Ineffective Boss to Brilliant Leader

Position Your Practice: A Guide for Women Working in Finance

SHIFT: How to Stand Out, Be Seen, and Grow Your Business With Integrity

SHIFT Success Journal

Publicity Action Plan Workbook: A Comprehensive Step-by-Step Workbook to Create a Complete Publicity Plan to Grow Your Business

Inspire: Women's Stories of Accomplishment, Encouragement and Influence

Empower: Women's Stories of Breakthrough, Discovery and Triumph

Inspired Entrepreneurs: A Collection of Female Triumphs in Business and Life

I Wish I'd Known That!: Secrets to Success in Business from Women Who've Been There

Please support independent booksellers. Books by Beth Caldwell are available at bookstores in the US, UK, Canada, and Australia. You can also purchase online at your favorite retailer. For bulk purchases or to invite Beth to speak to your book club, conference, or company, visit CoachBethCaldwell.com.

Let's Stay Connected

If you enjoyed reading Overcoming Imposter Syndrome, let's stay connected. I frequently offer online workshops, speak at conferences around the globe, and host in-person retreats that you may want to attend.

Sign up for my newsletter at **CoachBethCaldwell.com**

If you are into social media, follow me here:

instagram.com/beth_a_caldwell
or
linkedin.com/in/bethcaldwell

Seeing you post a photo of yourself reading this book will make my day. Be sure to tag me!